LIFE
BEFORE
DEATH

A STUDY OF
JUDGMENT &
ETERNAL LIFE
IN JOHN'S
GOSPEL

LIFE BEFORE DEATH

A STUDY OF
JUDGMENT &
ETERNAL LIFE
IN JOHN'S
GOSPEL

MATT HYAM

hopeful
INK
hI

LIFE BEFORE DEATH – A Study of Judgment and Eternal Life in John's Gospel

Copyright ©2018 Matt Hyam

All rights reserved. No part of this publication may be reproduced, distributed, or transmitted in any form or by any means, including photocopying, recording, or other electronic or mechanical methods, without the prior written permission of the publisher, except in the case of brief quotations embodied in critical reviews and certain other noncommercial uses permitted by copyright law.

ISBN 978-1-527232969

Published by Hopeful INK
Southampton, UK

Printed November 2018

Acknowledgments

Thank you, Dr Brad Jersak, for your incredible support, encouragement and wisdom in writing this thesis. But most especially for your friendship and for shining the light on the Scriptures to enable me to see Jesus instead of Molech.

Thank you, Georgina and the boys – Reuben, Sam, Nathaniel and George - for your patience with me. Gina, you can have your husband back now.

Thank you, Southampton Vineyard, for releasing me to study this MA and for being family to me for all these years.

CONTENTS

Chapter One
Introduction 1
    Relevance and Importance 1
    Contemporary Scholarship 1
    Primary Areas of Research 3
    Methodology and Outline 4

Chapter Two
An Examination of John 3:16 as a Distillation of the Gospel Announcement ... 8
    Why John 3:16? 8
    Love as the Foundation 9
    Believe (πιστευο - pistis) 10
    Eternal Life (αἰώνιος ζωή – aionios zoë) 13
    Perish (ἀπόλλυμι – appollumi) 16
    Reflection 20

Chapter Three
The Question of Κρίσις in the Fourth Gospel 21
    Contemporary Definitions 21
    The Septuagint 21
    Assumptions 22

Chapter Four
Κρίσις in John 3:17-21 23
    John 3:17 24
    John 3:18 25
    John 3:19 26
    John 3:20 30
    Reflection 31

Chapter Five
Κρίσις in John 5:21-30 34
    John 5:21-23 35
    John 5:24 36
    John 5:25-27 37
    John 5:28-30 39
    Reflection 40

Chapter Six
Κρίσις in John 12:44-50 43
    John 12:42,43 43
    John 12:44-46 45
    John 12:47,48 46
    John 12:49,50 47
    Reflection 48

Chapter Seven
Summary of Findings and Application 49
    John 3:16 and Αἰώνιος ζωή 50
    Κρίσις in the Gospel of John 51
    The Place of Αἰώνιος ζωή and Κρίσις in the Gospel Invitation ... 52

Bibliography 55

CHAPTER ONE

INTRODUCTION

Relevance and importance

Jesus invites us into *αἰώνιος ζωή* (*aionios zoë*) in John 3:16, but the nature of that offer is a source of much discussion among Christians – with views varying from a reward at the final judgment[1] to the *quality* of life today[2]. Investigating the offer of *αἰώνιος ζωή* in John's presentation of Jesus' words inevitably leads to addressing the corresponding warnings of *κρίσις* (*krisis*) for those who do not take up the offer. Again, the question revolves around the nature of *κρίσις* – what does it mean: is it just judgment *after* death? Is it judgment that is experienced now? Or is it a combination of both? And who faces it?

It seems that *αἰώνιος ζωή* and *κρίσις* are two sides of the same coin and attract the same examination, which will ultimately reveal the nature of the good news preached by Jesus and thus shape the good news preached by the church today. What is to be made of these differing understandings of *κρίσις* and *αἰώνιος ζωή*, and their bearing on evangelism?

Contemporary Scholarship

Grudem, among many others, specifically links judgment with Hell, which he defines as "a place of eternal conscious torment" and argues that this judgment is a "great motive for evangelism."[3] This is a widely held view within much of the Western church today and the "traditional view of the

---

[1] Wayne Grudem, *Systematic Theology: An Introduction to Biblical Doctrine* (IVP Press & Zondervan Publishing House, 1994), 1149.
[2] Dallas Willard, *The Divine Conspiracy* (Harper Collins, 1998), 40.
[3] Grudem, *Systematic Theology*, 1148.

Introduction

evangelical church,"[4] and while few would argue that seeking to save people from this is a worthy motive, an increasing number of scholars are questioning this emphasis in preaching and this understanding of judgment. Many prominent theologians and Bible Scholars including Brad Jersak,[5] Greg Boyd,[6] John Stott,[7] Karl Barth,[8] C.S. Lewis[9] and N.T. Wright,[10] disagree with this idea of the κρίσις, questioning Eternal Conscious Torment as the only "biblical" view of hell and, instead arguing for different understandings of judgment.

If we are to preach "the gospel," what place does the threat of *eternal* judgment have in it, and if saving people from eternal conscious torment is not the motivation, then what is? What are we seeking to see people saved from and to? Brian Zahnd points out that "in all the evangelistic sermons in the book of Acts, none of them makes an appeal to afterlife issues."[11] He goes on to assert that if one does not "know how to preach the gospel without making appeal to afterlife issues, you don't know how to preach the gospel!"[12] If we have preached a message that is about saving people from

---

[4] Evangelical Alliance Commision on Unity and Truth Among Evangelicals, *The Nature of Hell* (London: Paternoster, 2000), 2-4. Indeed, this report views other theologies to be "an immediate challenge to traditional evangelical understanding", 4.
[5] Bradley Jersak, *Her Gates Will Never Be Shut* (Wipf & Stock, 2009), 16.
[6] Greg Boyd, "Annihilation," *Dr. Platypus*, 21 Aug 2007, <https://pursiful.com/2007/08/21/greg-boyd-annihilation-or-eternal-suffering-1/> (7 Feb 2018).
[7] John Stott, "Judgement and Hell," *Truth According to Scripture*, n.d., <https://www.truthaccordingtoscripture.com/documents/death/judgement-hell.php#.WnsUk6hl_IU> (7 Feb 2018).
[8] Karl Barth, "The Extinction of Humanity: Karl Barth's Eschatology," *The PostBarthian*, 30 Nov 2016, <https://postbarthian.com/2016/11/30/extinction-humanity-karl-barths-eschatology/> (7 Feb 2018).
[9] Preston Sprinkle; John G. Stackhouse Jr, Robin A. Parry, Jerry L. Walls Denny Burk, *Four Views on Hell* (ed. Preston Sprinkle; : Zondervan, 2016) 9.
[10] Tom Wright, *Surprised by Hope* (London: SPCK, 2007) 187.
[11] Brian Zahnd, *Sinners in the Hands of a Loving God* (Waterbrook Press, 2017), 125.
[12] Zahnd, *Sinners*, 144.

hell and if, as Zahnd and the scholars above claim, that is not Jesus' message, where does that leave us and what *is* the message?

Primary Areas of Research

This thesis will focus on the presentation of the good news in the gospel of John, which I have chosen because John's gospel was "written that you may believe that Jesus is the Messiah, the Son of God, and that by believing you may have life in his name" (John 20:31, NIV). Douglas Moo, Leon Morris and Don Carson argue that, unlike the Synoptic gospels which were written to the church, "the Gospel of John was not written to believers *about* mission but to outsiders to *perform* mission."[13] Obviously, I do not in any way wish to diminish the message of judgment and eternal life in the Synoptic gospels, and a good argument could be given to focus on any one of those. Given the scope and length of this thesis it is not sensible to attempt to examine all of them in more than a superficial manner, and so I am suggesting that, as this is arguably the most universal of all four gospels[14] in its intended readership, my focus will be on John.

To complement the primary source of John's gospel, I will consult various other sources – academic commentaries on John, including Craig Keener, Leon Morris, D. A. Carson and Murray Harris; Greek-English Lexicons, including Walter Bauer for word studies; articles on the nature of

---

[13] Douglas J. Moo and Leon Morris D.A. Carson, *An Introduction to the New Testament* (Apollos, 1992) 171.

[14] Matthew focusses largely on the "connections between Jesus and his Old Testament Jewish Heritage", (Ralph P. Martin, *New Testament Foundations Vol.1* (Eerdmans, 1975), 225) and thus was largely aimed at a Jewish audience. Mark, whose "contents were largely embodied in the larger Gospels of Matthew and Luke" (Martin, *Foundations 1*, 178) "is either stated or implied in early traditions about the Gospel" was written in Rome for the Roman church (Douglas J. Moo and Leon Morris D.A. Carson, *An Introduction to the New Testament* (Appollos, 1992), 99. Luke "decided to write an orderly account for …most excellent Theophilus (Luke 1:3, NIV), who was possibly Luke's patron, although it seems likely that he intended it for a wider audience, probably "predominantly Gentile Christians" (*INT*, 118).

judgment and eschatology in John, including A.B Caneday and Alan Charles Blackwood; and patristic sources, including Augustine, Tertullian, Clement of Alexandria and Cyril of Alexandria.

Methodology and Outline

I will be focusing on the invitations to life and warnings of judgment in John's gospel and examine the use of language – specifically αἰώνιος ζωή and κρίσις – to better understand the message. I will also look at the context of each of these interactions where the presentation or warnings are given and, as much as possible, ascertain how they would have been understood at the time.

I will use the following outline and working chapter headings:

a. An Examination of John 3:16 as a Distillation of the Gospel Announcement in John.

This is an assumption, but I hope to show that it is not controversial[15], and there is merit for it. Jesus clearly presents an invitation to life and a warning for those who choose to reject it, offering αἰώνιος ζωή, what is required to receive it (πίστις - *pistis*) and the consequence of not choosing to receive it (ἀπόλλυμι).

- **The Nature and Understanding of πίστις.**
  - What does it mean to *believe*? The Oxford Dictionary definition of "believe" is "Accept that something is true, especially without proof" or "Hold (something) as an opinion."[16] It is highly questionable that this is what Jesus meant by πίστις and so it is vital to explore the meaning of the

---

[15] To which banners at sporting events worldwide will attest.
[16] Oxford Dictionaries, "Oxford Living Dictonaries," 2017, <https://en.oxforddictionaries.com> (16 November 2017)

word and how that should be understood in the New Testament (specifically in John's gospel).

- **The Nature and Understanding of *αἰώνιος ζωή*.**
    - As has been mentioned, there is much disagreement as to the meaning of *αἰώνιος*, and interesting to note that, in most translations of the Nicene Creed, "eternal life" is translated as "life *of* the world to come",[17] whereas a minority translate it as "life *in* the world to come."[18] This thesis will research this to ask whether Jesus was offering a quality of life, with implications in the age to come, or only offering life in the age to come.

- **The Nature and understanding of *ἀπόλλυμι*.**

    What does *ἀπόλλυμι* (*appollumi*) mean? Is *perishing* a fair translation and how is the word translated elsewhere in John and the other Gospels? Is it a threat or warning of something in the future or is it a recognition of a current situation?

b. **The Question of *Κρίσις* in the Fourth Gospel**

I have identified the three passages where *κρίσις* is discussed within the Fourth Gospel[19] and so will focus on those to explore the meaning. It would be easy to take any one of these passages and form a conclusion, but when they are examined in conjunction with each other they seem to create a far more complex picture than at first glance.

---

[17] Anglicans Online, "The Nicene Creed," *Anglicansonline.org*, May 2017, <http://anglicansonline.org/basics/nicene.html> (28 September 2017).
[18] Christian Reformed Church, "Nicene Creed," *Christian Reformed Church*, n.d., <https://www.crcna.org/welcome/beliefs/creeds/nicene-creed> (28 September 2017).
[19] There is a brief mention in 9:35-41, but I will not deal with this as it should be covered within the others.

c. *Κρίσις* in John 3:16-21

In this passage John appears to talk about ἀπόλλυμι as a state of humanity and Jesus offering life as an alternative, but this word is usually translated as "perishing" which appears to mean something distinct from *eternal conscious torment*. He goes on to contrast between light and darkness but seems to use the past tense in describing life and judgment. What does this mean? Has judgment *already* taken place?

d. *Κρίσις* in John 5:24-29

In this passage, there is a clear implication of future judgment, but Jesus appears to say that *all* will hear his voice and live (v.25). He goes on to say that he has been given the authority to judge (v.27) but if we contrast this with John 8:15, where he says that he does *not* pass judgment, then this raises more questions. In v.29, the dead are raised to life or judgment based on their deeds, which then begs further investigation, particularly as he has just appeared to have stated that *all* will live (v.25).

e. *Κρίσις* in John 12:44-50

Again, we see the contrast between light and darkness, but this time Jesus states that he does *not* judge those who do not keep his words, because he did not come to judge the world but to save it (v.47).

f. A Summary of Findings and Application

What are we left with as an understanding of "the gospel" according to John?

• What is the nature of the call for people to believe? How do we orientate church around this? What is our message?

• What is the life people are invited to? What does believing in Jesus look like? How do we help people to do this? Again, what is the message?

• What place does judgment play in preaching now? How do we present God? Is it a good reflection of Him or is it an image that turns people away? Is the warning, or even *threat*, of judgment a necessary or even helpful part of the message?

CHAPTER TWO

AN EXAMINATION OF JOHN 3:16 AS A DISTILLATION OF THE GOSPEL ANNOUNCEMENT IN JOHN

Why John 3:16?

"For God so loved the world that he gave his one and only Son, that whoever believes in him shall not perish but have eternal life." (John 3:16, NIV)

In looking at the nature of *judgment* and *eternal life* in John's Gospel, this verse seems to me the place to begin. It summarises much of what is expanded within the rest of the book, containing the motivation, means, response and consequences of the action of God through Christ. Beasley-Murray describes it as "the background canvas on which the rest of the gospel is painted."[20]

The context of the verse is a conversation between Jesus and Nicodemus, a member of the ruling classes. There seems to be a wide variety of views as to the character of Nicodemus – someone of "inadequate" faith or courage,[21] someone driven to speak to Jesus out of fear[22] or that he "represented both the more open-minded wing of the Sanhedrin and the Jewish nation as a whole in failing to comprehend the true significance of Jesus."[23] Jesus lays out what is required to be

---

[20] George Beasley-Murray, *John (2nd ed.)* (Nashville: Thomas Nelson, 1999), 51.
[21] Leon Morris, *The Gospel According to John* (Grand Rapids: Wm. B. Eermanns Publishing C., 1995), 104.
[22] Michaels, *John*, 55.
[23] Murray J. Harris, *John* (Nashville: B&H Academic, 2015), 72. It seems that, whatever his position at the time of this conversation, Nicodemus had become a follower by the time of Jesus' death (John 19:39).

his follower, challenging Nicodemus repeatedly in the process. Arguably, the discourse builds up and reaches its apex in 3:16 and then the following verses unpack it further.

Scholars agree[24] that the fourth gospel is punctuated by "meditations" [25] by the author, and that this verse may be one of them. Essentially, John seems to stop and reflect on what has been said, and in so doing seems to encapsulate his main thesis in one sentence.

Love as the Foundation

Undergirding this reflection is the concept of love, which the Gospel of John uses more than any other book in the Bible. It is no surprise, therefore, that John highlights the incredible love God has for his image-bearers as the motivation for his actions in saving humanity. Carson notes that "the Greek construction behind 'so loved that he gave his one and only son'… emphasises the intensity of the love."[26] Keener, similarly, notes that "John's language is qualitative rather than quantitative," translating the sentence as "this is *how* God loved the world."[27]

Perhaps we have become so used to hearing this phrase that we can lose the significance of "this… distinctively Christian idea that God's love is wide enough to embrace all people."[28] The Jewish people understood that God loved Israel,[29] but the idea that this love was not limited to them, is radical and unique. Morris goes on to stress that this love is not for the "spiritual elite" or, as "in recent times

---

[24] Morris, *John,* 202.
[25] D. A. Carson, *The Gospel According to John* (Leicester: Apollos, 1991), 203.
[26] Carson, *John,* 204.
[27] Craig S. Keener, *The Gospel of John - A commentary Volume 1* (Baker Academic, 2012), 566.
[28] Morris, *John,* 203.
[29] Morris, *John*, 203.

some scholars have argued… only for believers, but …it is plain that God loves 'the world'."[30] Carson notes that:

> "it is atypical for John to speak of God's love for *the world*, but this truth therefore is made to stand out as all the more wonderful… Jews were familiar with the truth that God loved the children of Israel; here God's love is not restricted by race… Christians are not to love the world with the selfish love of participation; God loves the world with the selfless, costly love of redemption."[31]

In any discussion about soteriology or eschatology, it is vital that the foundation is the love of God and its "ultimate expression," [32] Christ's sacrifice on the cross. It is easy to become focused on the dynamics and the different theological views and miss the whole point that it was *all* because "God so loved the world." With love underpinning this passage we are then able to move on and explore the rest of the verse. I will specifically focus on the words *believe*, *eternal life* and *perish* as the means and promise of receiving the love of God, and consequence of rejecting it.

"This is how God loved the world, he gave the gift of his one and only son…"

Believe (πιστευο)

As mentioned before, the Oxford Dictionary defines "believe" as, "Accept that something is true, especially without proof" or "Hold (something) as an opinion."[33] This understanding is a typically western view, which is essentially cognitive in its nature.[34] This assumption has crept into the church and distorted our understanding

---

[30] Morris, *John*, 203.
[31] Carson, *John*, 204.
[32] Keener, *John 1*, 566.
[33] Oxford Dictionaries, "Oxford Living Dictonaries," 2017, <https://en.oxforddictionaries.com> (16 November 2017).
[34] 300 years before Christ, Plato saw πίστις as "the lowest form of epistemic state" and "the sorts of second-hand, uninformed views that people hold." Michael Lacewing, "Plato's

of the good news, because "to *believe*" has come to mean that we agree with the facts. We sign statements of *belief* to say that we agree with certain assertions in order to be considered safe to speak or to be endorsed by an organisation.[35]

Keener points out that "modern readers of John 3:15-16 who assume that it rewards passive faith with eternal life, apart from perseverance, read these verses in accordance with a very modern theological understanding that is utterly foreign to their Johannine context."[36]

With this template placed over John 3:16, *to believe in Jesus* means that we agree with a number of statements about him. This may be true. We *may* agree with those statements but that is not what John is asking of us and there is a danger of us selling the gospel short by reducing his meaning and reinterpreting vital statements such as John 3:16.

If *believe* does not merely mean "to agree with" or "to hold an opinion", what *does* it mean, particularly in this context? The "Greek-English Lexicon of the New Testament and Other Early Christian Literature" defines πιστευο as "that which causes faith or trust" or "trust, confidence, faith,"[37] while the NASB Dictionary defines it as "faith, faithfulness."[38] Harris notes that πιστευο appears in the Fourth Gospel ninety-eight times and that John uses it in a specific way – "believe *in*" –

Similies of the Cave and the Divided Line," *Routledge*, n.d., <http://documents.routledge-interactive.s3.amazonaws.com/9781138793934/A2/Plato/PlatoSimilesLineCave.pdf> (9 Feb 2018). By New Testament times it had come to mean something far richer.

[35] Last summer I was asked, by a student group, to sign a statement of faith (essentially a collection of points). Failure to do so meant that our church would not be promoted by the group.

[36] Keener, *John 1*, 570.

[37] Walter Bauer, *A Greek-English Lexicon of the New Testament and Other Early Christian LIterature* (ed. William F. Arndt and F. Wilbur Gingrich; Chicago: Univeristy of Chicago Press, 1979), 662.

[38] R. L. Thomas, *New American Standard Hebrew-Aramaic and Greek Dictionaries: updated Edition* (Anaheim: Foundation Publications, inc., 1998).

which only rarely occurs outside this book, and he uses it "only of a divine object of faith... [almost always] Christ."[39]

In the light of this, I assert that we can define *"believe in Jesus"* as *to put our trust, confidence or faith in Jesus*, which is a radical departure from merely agreeing with statements and the "passive faith"[40] critiqued by Keener above. Having a good understanding of what it means to *believe* is critical to every aspect of our faith. Like Keener, I fear that by applying a modern understanding of "believe" we not only water down, but utterly alter the invitation. It is the difference between winning *converts* and making *disciples* and thus, must necessarily shape our evangelism and our ecclesiology. If we only ask people to agree with things *about* Jesus, and not be transformed *by* Him, then we can rob them of the very life they are promised and can end up giving people a religion that could inoculate them against Jesus.

Even with this definition, one can still reasonably ask the question as to what "putting our trust or confidence in Jesus" would look like in actuality. Morris describes it as "spiritual change wherein one ceases to rely on one's own merits and achievements and comes to trust in Christ instead,"[41] and Harris defines it still further, stating:

> "The... phrase 'believe in' depicts the total committal of one's total self to the person of Christ as Messiah and Lord, something more than an intellectual acceptance of the message of the gospel and a recognition of the truth about Christ, although these aspects are involved. For John,

---

[39] Harris, *John*, 31. He notes that in only two occurrences does John use this of God (12:44 and 14:1) but that the rest are of Christ."
[40] Keener, *John 1*, 570.
[41] Morris, *John*, 88.

belief involves not only recognition and acceptance of truth but also adherence and allegiance to Jesus *as the Truth* [emphasis mine]."[42]

This is a good working definition of what is required of us in believing in Jesus, more akin to a baby or a toddler, totally trusting and dependent upon a parent for everything than to a contractual agreement over some facts about parenting. John calls us to be totally trusting and child-like in our acceptance of Jesus and to hand over *everything* of ourselves to his loving care.

"This is how God loved the world, he gave the gift of his one and only son, that whoever gives themselves over to him, totally…"

Eternal Life *(αἰώνιος ζωή)*

The Oxford Dictionary defines *eternal* as "lasting or existing forever; without end."[43] A modern rendering of *eternal life* would therefore logically be *life forever*. It seems, in much popular Christian thinking this is often understood as a "destiny"[44] or life *after* death. One website states clearly that "all people will have eternal life. It is just a matter of where you spend it – heaven or hell."[45] Going back to Keener's point about modern readers[46], the question must be asked whether the contemporary understanding of *eternal* (and thus *eternal life*) is legitimate in trying to ascertain what it is that Jesus is saying, and thus the

---

[42] Harris, *John*, 32.
[43] *Oxford Living Dictionary*.
[44] John Piper, "The Destiny: Eternal Life," *Desiring God*, 25 Dec 1994,
<https://www.desiringgod.org/messages/the-destiny-eternal-life> (24 Jan 2018). To be fair to Piper, he does explain that *eternal life* begins now, but the title clearly stating it as a destiny sends a definite message.
[45] Eternal Life, "Eternal Life," *All About Spirituality* , n.d.,
<https://www.allaboutspirituality.org/eternal-life-faq.htm> (24 Jan 2018). Again, the article does talk about eternal life beginning *now* but the main thrust is all about where one will be after they die.
[46] Keener, *John 1*, 570.

implications thereof. Westcott, for example, clearly states that the phrase *eternal life* should be "distinguished from *life forever*." [47]

It certainly appears that the concept of *eternal life* is particularly, if not exclusively, Johannine[48], and Morris notes that the word *αἰώνιος* appears in the Fourth Gospel 17 times, which is "nearly three times as often as in any other New Testament book" and is "always in this Gospel used of life." Keener observes that *ζωή* appears thirty-six times in John's Gospel and letters, claiming that "even when not conjoined with 'eternal,' the term designates eternal life…"[49]

He points to a Jewish worldview, and thus an understanding of *eternal life* as "'life of the world to come'…or 'life of the age,'" which seems in line with how the Nicene Creed interprets the phrase.[50] He does, however, state that John's gospel "employs the term somewhat differently from contemporary Jewish sources and the Synoptics. Linking it with present-tense verbs, the Fourth Gospel declares that the life of the kingdom era is available to those living in the present…"[51] In fact, John 17:3 directly defines 'eternal life' in the present in relationship to knowing God and the sent Son *now*.

Similarly noting a Jewish eschatological view of time being divided into the "present age and the age to come", Morris suggests that *eternal* "means 'pertaining to an age,'" Similarly, Ramelli and Konstan conclude that it is best rendered as "pertaining to the future world,"[52], but is clear that "the important thing about

---

[47] Brooke Foss Westcott, *The Gospel According to St John* , 54. He defines *eternal* as "not an endless duration of being in time but being of which time is not a measure."[47] Brooke Foss Westcott, *The Epistles of St John* , 214.
[48] Wescott, *Gospel,* 54.
[49] Keener, *John 1,* 328.
[50] Anglicans Online, *Nicene Creed.* Although, it should be noted that the "Christian Reformed Church", for example, have translated the phrase as "life *in* the age to come", thus changing the meaning to suit a "life after death" interpretation.
https://www.crcna.org/welcome/beliefs/creeds/nicene-creed.
[51] Keener, *John 1,* 328.
[52] Ilaria L. E. Ramelli & David Konstan, *Terms for Eternity: Aionios and Aidios in Classical and Christian Texts* (Piscataway: Gorgias Press LLC, 2013), 104.

eternal life is not its quantity but its quality."[53] Salmond describes *eternal life* as "a qualitative or ethical conception" which he defines as, "the new condition…the life that fulfils the whole idea of life, the good life, the perfection of life, the satisfaction of life in God… it lies in the nature of the life as *eternal*, life of the divine order…"[54]

Michaels makes the claim that *eternal life* in John is "this Gospel's equivalent of the Kingdom of God" and is clear that it is "not simply endless life; nor is it a life that begins after death. It is a new *kind* of life, a new order of existence that characterises even now the person who believes in Jesus…"[55] Caneday likewise states that "eternal life, which properly belongs to the coming age, is already present with the incarnation of the Word and is now being imparted to all who believe in God's Son."[56] In "The Divine Conspiracy," Dallas Willard makes a similar assertion, devoting an entire chapter to "The Eternal *Kind* of Life," stating that, "the person of Jesus …makes it possible for us to translate our 'ordinary' life into an eternal one."[57]

As we gather all these views together we can see that *eternal life* is a *kind* of life that we can both look forward to, but, significantly, experience right now.[58] This kind of life "has nothing to do with circumstances. Life means we are really alive, even if we have nothing. Life means that it doesn't matter whether we are in prison for our faith, permanently sick, on the streets begging or living luxuriously

---

[53] Morris, *John*, 201.
[54] Stewart D. F. Salmond, *The Christian Doctrine of Immortality* (Edinburgh: T. & T. Clark, 1901), 391.
[55] J. Ramsey Michaels, *John* (Massachusetts: Hendrickson, 1989), 59.
[56] A. B. Caneday, "The Advent of God's Son as Judgement in John's Gospel: Justification and Condemnation Already," *Credo Magazine*, November 2011,
<http://www.credomag.com/wp-content/uploads/2011/11/The-Advent-of-God%E2%80%99s-Son-as-Judgment-in-John%E2%80%99s-Gospel-Justification-and-Condemnation-Already.pdf> (16 November 2017), 5.
[57] Willard, *Conspiracy*, 40.
[58] It should be noted that the tense for "have [eternal life]" is *present* tense.

in a mansion. Real life has everything to do with being satisfied with knowing God."[59]

Jesus' invitation was not to a future hope for things to be okay one day, but to a present hope that you can have fullness of life now, even amid the injustice and hardship. *Real* life is available to us right now - the life of the age to come that we were created to live, in the very first place.

"This is how God loved the world: he gave the gift of his one and only son, that whoever gives themselves over to him, totally... will have entered into the eternal kind of life from the coming age."

Perish *(ἀπόλλυμι)*

The Oxford Dictionary defines *perish* as "Die, especially in a violent or sudden way" and "suffer complete ruin or destruction."[60] *Perishing* is presented in John's gospel as the result of not choosing *eternal life.* So, on one level, this seems very straightforward – life or death – or as Morris asserts – "John sets perishing and life starkly over against one another.[61] Likewise, Carson points out that, "the alternative [to being saved] is to perish..., to lose one's life..., to be doomed to destruction... There is no third option."[62] Keener takes it further by stating that "'perishing' applied naturally to physical destruction, but already had long appeared in early Christian texts for eternal destruction."[63]

On the face of it, unlike *believe* and *eternal,* a modern reading of *perish* would appear to render the same meaning. Indeed, the "Greek-English Lexicon of the

---

[59] Matt Hyam, *I Still Have More Questions Than Answers* (Vineyard International Publishing, 2004), 77.
[60] *Oxford Living Dictionary.*
[61] Morris, *John,* 204.
[62] Carson, *John,* 206.
[63] Keener, *John 1,* 570. He does, however, offer no explanation of how *eternal* should be understood in the context of *eternal destruction*. If one were to take his approach towards *eternal life* and use it here, then *eternal destruction* would be expected to mean "destruction of the kingdom era." I am not sure how this differs from *death* in this context.

New Testament and Early Christian Writings" defines ἀπόλλυμι primarily as, "ruin, destroy."[64] Thus, the simplest understanding of John 3:16 in this context is that, to not believe means death, which suggests a clear argument for an *annihilationist*[65] eschatology.

However, I want to suggest that this is not as straightforward as it would seem. While Bauer gives the first meaning as "ruin, destroy," another meaning of ἀπόλλυμι is "lost." The root of the word, according to the NASB Dictionary, is ἀπό, which it defines as "from, away from"[66] and Bauer notes is the root of "all verbs expressing the idea of separation."[67]

In fact, the word ἀπόλλυμι occurs 66 times in the four gospels, and in 38 of those occurrences, it is normally translated as *lost* (Matt 10:6, 15:24; Luke 15:4-9 etc.). In John's Gospel, ἀπόλλυμι appears ten times and in the NIV, three times it is translated as *perish* (3:16, 10:28, 11:50), four times *lost* (17:12, 18:9, 6:39, 12:25), once *destroy* (10:10), once *wasted* (6:12)[68] and once as *spoil* (6:27). If we focus on the times when it is translated as *perish,* I want to argue that there is a case for *lost* being at least as good a translation, if not better.

"My sheep listen to my voice; I know them, and they follow me. I give them eternal life, and they shall never *be lost*; no one will snatch them out of my hand." (10:28) Given that the idea of having the sheep "snatched" means *losing* them and we see the motif of *lost* sheep[69] in two of the other Gospels, *perish* seems a strange translation. Four of the five mentions of "lost" in Matthew and Luke are to do with sheep and so is it such a stretch to suggest that John had similar stories in mind,

---

[64] Bauer, *Lexicon,* 95.
[65] This is a view whereby it is believed that "terminal punishment is the view of hell most warranted by Scripture." (John G. Stackhouse Jr, *Four View on Hell,* 62.
[66] Thomas, *NASB Dictionary.*
[67] Bauer, *Lexicon,* 86.
[68] This is the clearing up after feeding the 5000 and refers to nothing being *wasted* from the leftovers. Arguably, *lost* would work as well.
[69] The "parable of the dead sheep" does not seem to convey the same meaning.

having heard them from Jesus first hand? If this is the case, then *perish* rather than *lost* seems an even more strange rendering.[70]

"Then one of them, named Caiaphas, who was high priest that year, spoke up, "You know nothing at all! You do not realize that it is better for you that one man die for the people than that the whole nation *be lost*." (11:49,50) The Pharisees have just expressed their fear that the Romans will "take away both our temple and our nation" (48) – their nation and temple would be *lost* - and I would argue that the more *obvious* translation would then be *lost*, not *perish*, because, from my reading of the text, to use *perish* would seem to introduce a new concept out of nowhere.

That leaves us with the only other occurrence of ἀπόλλυμι being translated as *perish* in John, which is John 3:16. If ἀπόλλυμι can mean *perish* or *lost* then there needs to be a good reason to consider translating it as *lost* instead of *perish*, particularly in defiance of such revered and learned theologians.

Even with all the scholars that I have looked at, there are still a couple of things puzzling me. First, arguably, the general consensus is that the gift of *eternal life* is received now, but if *perish* means what it seems, the consequence of turning down *life now* is death *later*. This seems a strange offer. You can have this gift now but if you refuse it, you will be punished in the future. This is incongruous. Where does that leave people who have not believed but not yet died? Are they dead or alive? That suggests a third option, even though most of the scholars above insisted on only two – to be alive, but not with *eternal* life.

The interesting thing about all the passages concerning lost (ἀπόλλυμι) things in Matthew and Luke is that the lost thing is *already* in a state of being lost, *until* it has been saved. For this reason, I suggest that *lost* is a better translation of

---

[70] While *perish* does not work as a metaphor for *lost* the inverse is true and *lost* does work as a metaphor for *perishing*.

John 3:16

ἀπόλλυμι in John 3:16,[71] unless the word *perish* is used in the context of the people *already* perishing from the snake bites. The implication, in this case, would be that all of humanity is in a pre-existing state of *being lost* or *perishing*, but those who *believe* will no longer be *perishing,* but will have *eternal life* and, taken in the context of 3:14-15, this is the only sensible conclusion.[72]

This brings me to my second concern. None of the scholars that I found make any reference to the preceding verses, in which John recounts the story from Numbers 21, which should *surely* inform our interpretation of v.16 as it is there for a very good reason. When Moses lifted up the snake on the pole, people were *already* in a state of sickness from snake bites (which Augustine states are analogous to, "sins, from the mortality of the flesh")[73] and if they looked upon it, they were delivered from this condition. The sickness, which was a consequence of their sin, was not a consequence of *not* looking upon it and will only result in death if they refuse to look upon it. The parallel is made for us between the snake lifted by Moses and Jesus on the cross, so how can we then step into the next verse and interpret it otherwise? Humanity is lost to a sickness that is killing us and we are offered life if we will trust Jesus. As Augustine continues, "so far, then, as it lies in the physician, He has come to heal the sick. He that will not observe the orders of the physician destroys himself."[74]

Salmond states, "'death' is the ethical condition, the condition of failure and evil in which men exist by nature, and out of which they are raised by Christ"[75] The invitation in John 3:16 is an invitation to be *raised* out of death, *not a threat of death* to those who refuse it. Morris makes the point "they... perish because they

---

[71] David Bentley Hart, *The New Testament: A Translation* (New Haven: Yale University Press, 2017), 174.
[72] "Perish" here is in the *aorist tense*, which is a form of *past* tense, and further lends to this assertion.
[73] Augustine, "Tractate 12," *New Advent*, 2017,
<http://www.newadvent.org/fathers/1701012.htm> (24 Jan 2018), 11.
[74] Augustine, Tractate 12, 12.
[75] Salmond, *Immortality,* 391.

prefer darkness to light"[76] People are in the darkness *already* which John attests to in verses 19-21 (which we will examine further in the next chapter). The invitation in John 3:16 is an invitation to come out of the darkness into the light, *not a threat of darkness* for those who refuse it.

> *"This is how God loved the world, he gave the gift of his one and only son, that whoever gives themselves over to him, totally will no longer be perishing but will have entered into the eternal kind of life from the coming age."*

Reflection

John 3:16 summarises the gospel message in the Fourth Gospel, which is one of invitation to leave a way of life that is killing us, one that has us lost and our souls dead, and to enter into a way of life that is the life we were made to live. A life that is a foretaste of the age to come. A life of fullness now, before the world has been restored.

Too often, John 3:16 is presented as a threat or ultimatum when it is actually a beautiful invitation. We see it as the warning of punishment, when it is the offer of rescue. The creator of the universe showed his incredible love for us by giving us his own son so that we can be freed from slavery. All we are asked to do is to believe – to *trust* – in Jesus.

---

[76] Morris, *John*, 202. I am fairly sure that he would not appreciate me using his quote to dispute his position.

CHAPTER THREE

THE QUESTION OF *ΚΡΙΣΙΣ* IN THE FOURTH GOSPEL

Contemporary Definitions

In contemporary translations, *κρίσις* is most often rendered as "judged" or "condemned", both of which carry specific connotations. The Oxford Dictionary defines "to judge" as "form an opinion or conclusion about", "decide (a case) in a law court", "give a verdict on (someone) in a law court", or "decide the results of (a competition)." It defines "to condemn" as "express complete disapproval of", "sentence (someone) to a particular punishment", "force (someone) to endure or accept something unpleasant", or "prove or show to be guilty or unsatisfactory."[77]

Even a cursory overview of these definitions creates some questions because, while there is clearly a small amount of overlap in that they can both be used in a legal setting, the two words appear to mean something very different from each other. One, it seems, is about making a decision or evaluating, whereas the other is about inflicting something upon a person – be it punishment or disapproval. The idea that the two could be interchangeable in the English translations ought to raise some concerns.

The Septuagint

A look at the Septuagint shows that, within the Torah, the use of *κρίσις* almost always refers to decision making – often in a legal setting between two people where the judge is *evaluating* the situation and *deciding* who is right or wrong.[78]

---

[77] *Oxford Living Dictionaries.*
[78] Exod 22:9, 25:14; Deut 5:6, 17, 17:8. On some occasions the idea of the role of *evaluating/decision-making* seems to overlap or be synonymous with *ruling*. It is interesting

There appears to be very little usage of it to denote punishment[79] and so I suggest that we have perhaps retrospectively read the punishment motif into it by reading through modern lenses.

Assumptions

There is a common Western Reformed view prevalent within Evangelical circles, that sin is a crime that *must* be punished.[80] However, this is very different from the view of the Early Church Fathers, such as Athanasius, who saw sin is a sickness that needed a cure.[81] If one assumes the former view, as many Evangelicals do, we put on lenses that read "judgment" in a condemnatory or punitive fashion, whereas the latter view, held by many of the early church, gives a very different reading. Even a doctor makes *judgments* in diagnosing an illness, and even a prognosis of death is not punishment, so I think it is a mistake to *assume* the idea of condemnation, especially in the light of the passage we have just discussed (3:14,15), which outlines the scenario in Numbers where the snake on the pole is the *cure* for the snake venom and not a punishment.

Let us, then, try to set aside an assumption of condemnation or punishment as we read *κρίσις* in these passages and see whether we come to the same conclusions or that the context will reveal something else.

---

to note that the word is used for "the distinguishing thing" of a Priest (Deut 5:23). *Κρίνω* appears three times and is used to mean "judge", "rule" or "ruling" (Gen 15:14, 18:25, Deut 25:1).

[79] Gen 15:14 may be the exception to this as it refers to YHWH *judging* Egypt, although it is also arguable that the condemnation interpretation is reading something into the original understanding. It would be just as valid to translate it as YHWH *evaluating* Egypt in the light of their treatment of Israel.

[80] Grudem, *Systematic,* 501. See also; John Piper, "Are All Sins Equal Before God?," *Desiring God*, 2 Nov 2009, <https://www.desiringgod.org/interviews/are-all-sins-equal-before-god> (1 February 2018).

[81] Athanasius of Alexandria, *On the Incarnation* (Fig books, 2012) 6, 14. See also Augustine, *Tractate 12:12* quoted in previous chapter.

CHAPTER FOUR

ΚΡΙΣΙΣ IN JOHN 3:17-21

"Just as Moses lifted up the serpent in the desert, so it is necessary for the Son of Man to be lifted up, that everyone having faith in him might have the life of the Age. For God so loved the cosmos as to give the Son, the only one, so that everyone having faith in him might not perish but have the life of the Age. For God sent the Son into the cosmos not that he might pass judgment on the cosmos, but that the cosmos might be saved through him. Whoever has faith in him is not judged; whoever does not have faith has already been judged, because he has not had faith in the name of the only Son of God. And this is the judgment, that the light has come into the cosmos, and men loved the darkness rather than the light because their deeds were wicked. For everyone who does evil things hates the light and does not approach the light, for fear his deeds will be exposed. But whoever acts in truth approaches the light, so that his deeds might be made manifest – that they have been worked in God." - John 3:15-21[82]

I have included the three preceding verses to provide the context for the passage we are examining as I think it is vital for us to have the Numbers 21 narrative in view. John ascribes this importance to the words of Jesus, beginning both v.16 and 17 with *γάρ,* which is a "conjunction used to express cause, inference, continuation, or to explain."[83] We must, therefore, treat the verses that follow as the *point* of Jesus quoting the Numbers passage because the text tells us

---

[82] David Bentley Hart, *The New Testament: A Translation* (New Haven: Yale University Press, 2017), 174.
[83] Bauer, *Lexicon*, 151.

to. As such, we keep in mind Moses raising up the serpent among people who are suffering and dying from snake venom.

John 3:17

"For God sent the Son into the cosmos not that he might pass judgment on the cosmos, but that the cosmos might be saved through him."

The statement of verse 17 that Jesus was not sent to judge is in apparent contradiction of later passages in the same gospel, particularly 9:39, but Harris argues that the very presence of Jesus forced people "to accept or reject him," and that those who rejected him "had passed judgment on themselves."[84] Morris argues that judgment and salvation are "two sides to the one coin" and that "salvation for those who believe implies judgment on all who do not."[85]

Carson, however, asserts that "he did not come into a neutral world in order to save some and condemn others; he came into a lost world in order to save some."[86] And Keener, likewise, says that "in John's theology, the world is condemned already" which he states is "consonant with Early Christian soteriology."[87] Certainly this view resonates with Athanasius: "[God] pitying our race, moved with compassion… unable to endure that death should have the mastery… that his creatures should perish…, He took to Himself a human body…"[88] Perhaps more importantly, this views fits into the Numbers 21 narrative. The serpent on the pole did not condemn or judge but offered healing and salvation from the death that was in control.

---

[84] Harris, *John,* 79.
[85] Morris, *John,* 205.
[86] Carson, *John,* 207. One should want to question the "some" in that statement because "some" is not the same as "the cosmos."
[87] Keener, *John 1,* 570.
[88] Athanasius, *Incarnation 7,* 17.

Keener goes on to point out how the idea of God coming to rescue us was a radical and "distinctive position in Mediterranean antiquity of the period" where, "by contrast, pagans often feared that the gods would abandon the world because of its wickedness…; Jewish people feared that the Shekinah could withdraw for the same reason."[89] The idea that YHWH would step into the world *because* of the mess and at enormous cost, bring healing and restoration, in contrast to the prevailing views, gives us insight in the incredible significance of John 3:17.

John 3:18

"Whoever has faith in him is not judged; whoever does not have faith has already been judged, because he has not had faith in the name of the only Son of God."

Harris argues that the first sentence of v.18 should be translated as, "is not (now) under a sentence of condemnation." In other words, they have stepped out of the sentence by believing. By contrast, one who does not believe "(already) stands condemned" and "the judgment of the Last Day will confirm a verdict of self-judgment already passed." [90]

Chrysostom states that "he either means that disbelief itself is the punishment for the impenitent …or he is announcing beforehand what is to be. Even if a murderer is not yet sentenced by the judge, still his crime has condemned him."[91] The former is close to the view of Irenaeus, who argues that it is not God who brings κρίσις, but that it is self-inflicted and self-fulfilling.

> "…in the case of a flood of light: those who have blinded themselves, or have been blinded by others, are forever deprived of the

---

[89] Keener, *John 1*, 571.
[90] Harris, *John*, 79. This idea of the judgment being self-inflicted is echoed by Morris, *John*, 206.
[91] Chrysostom, John; Joel C. Elowsky, ed., *Ancient Christian Commentary on Scripture, New Testament IVa, John 1-10* (Illinois: IVP, 2006), 127.

enjoyment of light. It is not, [however], that the light has inflicted upon
them the penalty of blindness, but it is that the blindness itself has
brought calamity upon them: and therefore the Lord declared, 'He that
believeth in Me is not condemned.'"[92]

The breadth of views here leaves us in danger of becoming more confused about what this *κρίσις* is than when we started. Are we talking about a future condemnation or a present judgment? Is that judgment imposed upon us or self-inflicted? What is the nature of that judgment? Salmond argues that "the Fourth Gospel certainly speaks of the judgment more as a present process…"[93]

Again, we need to go back to look at vv.14,15 and then review 18 in the light of that. The view of *κρίσις* stated by Irenaeus seems to closely parallel this narrative and seems to make the most sense if we strip away the *condemnation* prejudice and read within context and with an open mind. The following verse will bring more clarity to this argument.

John 3:19

"And this is the judgment, that the light has come into the cosmos, and men loved the darkness rather than the light because their deeds were wicked."

Before we go any further, let us pause and look at the first word of this sentence; *δέ*. The word means "*but*, when a contrast is clearly implied; *and*, when a simple connective is desired."[94] There is a *connective* at the start of v.19, which means that it is to be taken together with v.18. If we put the two together we should be able to see something. "Whoever has faith in him is not *κρίνεται*;

---

[92] Irenaeus, "Irenaeus: Against Heresies," *The Gnostic Society Library*, n.d., <http://gnosis.org/library/advh5.htm> (31 January 2018), Book 5; 27:2.
[93] Salmond, *Immortality*, 260.
[94] Bauer, *Lexicon*, 171.

whoever does not have faith has already been *κρίνεται*, because he has not had faith in the name of the only Son of God. And *this is the κρίσις*...

If we take the two together, we can clearly see how, in v.19, John *clarifies* the nature of the *κρίσις* described in v.18 – "this is what that *κρίσις* is." It is somewhat disturbing to note that many modern translations use two different words for the translation of *κρίσις* – one (usually "condemned") in v.18 and another (usually "judgment") in v.19.[95] This renders it impossible to read v.19 as an explanation of v.18, effectively dismisses the connective, making the two verses totally separate and preventing the reader from seeing the relevance.

Morris critiques the NIV translation as "misleading" and argues that John "is telling us how the process works. People choose the darkness and their condemnation lies in that very fact."[96] Cyril of Alexandria seemed to hold a similar view, stating that; "they…who when it was in their power to be illuminated preferred to remain in darkness, how will not they fairly be determiners of punishment against themselves, and self-invited to suffering which it was in their power to escape." [97]

Carson states that "the 'darkness' in John is not only absence of light, but positive evil" but Keener disagrees, arguing that, while some Jewish sources use "darkness and light figuratively for evil and good," this view actually creates a "gnostic background" and "Jewish teachers applied light and darkness imagery to a variety of specific occasions, all of which reflect a common appreciation for the goodness of light and a common disdain for the dangers of darkness."[98] Essentially, the light, which is connected with the day, reveals things, enabling us

---

[95] See NIV, ESV, NRSV, RSV.
[96] Morris, *John,* 207.
[97] Cyril of Alexandria, "Commentary on John, Book 2," *The Tertullian Project*, 2005, <http://www.tertullian.org/fathers/cyril_on_john_02_book2.htm> (16 November 2017).
[98] Keener, *John 1,* 385.

to see the way, to see things as they are and to see the truth, whereas the darkness, which is connected to the night, leaves us vulnerable and blind.

If v.19 *defines* the *κρίσις* of v.18 then arguably the fact that people remain trapped in the darkness unable to enjoy the freedom of the light is the *κρίσις* itself, and not what leads to the *κρίσις*. This would fit with the Number 21 narrative, where one would choose to not look up at the serpent and to stay looking down, dying from snake venom.

In his book, "the Last Battle", C. S. Lewis tells the story of the final days of Narnia in which the people are deceived and led astray into false worship and many turn away from their faith. Much of the story revolves around a stable where Aslan is rumoured to be staying, although it is really a con featuring a donkey in a lion's skin. This stable has become a place of evil with the Calormene god Tash appearing from within it. Towards the end of the story there is a battle and the children are being pushed back to the stable. They have already seen several dwarfs, who had turned away from Aslan, tied up and thrown into it as punishment by the evil Calormene ruler, and eventually they themselves end up through the doorway. To their surprise, they open their eyes to see that they are in the New Narnia which is astonishingly beautiful, full of delight and wonder.

After a time, they spot the dwarfs who are no longer bound but sitting in a tight circle facing one another. The children try to speak to them, but the dwarves behave very strangely.

> "'Look out!' said one of the them in a surly voice, 'Mind where you're going. Don't walk into our faces!'
>
> 'All right!' said Eustace indignantly. 'We're not blind. We've got eyes in our heads.'
>
> 'They must be darn good ones if you can see in here,' said the same dwarf whose name was Diggle.

> 'In where?' asked Edmund.
>
> 'Why you bonehead, in *here* of course,' said Diggle.
>
> 'But it isn't dark, you poor stupid Dwarfs," said Lucy.
>
> 'Can't you see? Look up! Look round! Can't you see *me*?'
>
> 'How in the name of all Humbug can I see what ain't there? And how can I see you anymore than you can see me in this pitch darkness?'...
>
> ... 'There is no black hole, save in your own fancy, fool,' cried Tirian. 'Come out of it.' And leaning forward, he caught Diggle by the belt and hook and swung him right out of the circle of Dwarfs. But the moment Tirian put him down, Diggle darted back to his place among the others..."[99]

This is *κρίσις*. The light was there. Beauty surrounded them. Sights and sounds and smells and tastes to savour. They were free; no longer bound by their cords, and yet they were living as though they were tied up in a pitch-black stable. Unable to believe, and stuck in darkness when there was light all around. Even when an attempt is made to free them from their self-imposed prison, they choose to run back to the security of their blindness.

Jesus is speaking to one of the religious leaders of Israel and talking about being bound up in the darkness because they refuse to see the light. The light/dark imagery cannot be coincidental when looked at in conjunction with the phrase "Nicodemus came to him *at night,*"[100] and the connection between dark and night. John seems to be making the point that Jesus is likening the Sanhedrin to those in darkness, refusing to come to the light and their judgment is that they sit there

---

[99] C. S. Lewis, *The Last Battle* (Glasgow: Fontana Lions, 1956), 137-139.
[100] John 3:2.

bound by their own refusal to trust. Jesus seems to reinforce his critique on the religious leaders as he continues.

John 3:20

"For everyone who does evil things hates the light and does not approach the light, for fear his deeds will be exposed. But whoever acts in truth approaches the light, so that his deeds might be made manifest – that they have been worked in God."

Carson states that "the person who loves the darkness practices evil…"[101] which reiterates his view that the darkness is in some way a source of evil. Michaels, however, argues that staying in the darkness is *because* of their evil deeds.[102] This latter view seems to hold more with Keener's assertion that darkness was not a metaphor for evil[103] but the place of hiding evil deeds and vulnerability *to* evil.

The one who was doing evil would not approach the light, *for fear his deeds will be exposed.* Keener asserts that Jesus, in saying this to Nicodemus and who he represents of the Jewish leaders, was confronting "the character they already have."[104] John must be equating those *who do evil things and will not come to the light* with the religious leaders, who were the only people in Israel who refused to come to him. Even Gentiles[105] and Samaritans (John 4) came to him before the priests and Pharisees would.

To illustrate, I have four sons. Like most boys, their behaviour occasionally[106] slips from *purely* angelic into some minor transgressions. On even rarer occasions

---

[101] Carson, *John,* 208.
[102] Michaels, *John*, 59.
[103] Keener, *John 1,* 385.
[104] Keener, *John 1,* 572.
[105] Even Roman commanding officers – Matt 8, 27; Mark 15; Luke 7; 23.
[106] By which I mean several times an hour.

they may do something really bad that causes lasting damage to property or person. Sometimes, when they have done this, particularly when the destruction has yet to be discovered, they will try to pretend nothing has happened and avoid their parents because they fear being disciplined.[107]

This is what Jesus is saying. He is essentially accusing those who avoid the light (Nicodemus and those like him) of being wayward children who are too afraid to face up to what they have done. Their pride prevents them from coming to the light. The implication of this is that they *know* they are doing evil and do not want to admit it or have it seen for what it is. The religious leaders who profess to godliness and purport to lead the people of Israel in their faith *know* that they have another agenda and fear it being exposed.[108]

By contrast, he commends those who "do the truth"[109] for coming into the light so that their deeds can be seen plainly. As Tertullian puts it, "What is good... (provided it is true and full), does not love darkness: it rejoices in being seen and exults over the very recognition it receives."[110] People who are able to humble themselves will come without fear, knowing that they will be healed, just as those who would look to the serpent on the pole will be healed.

Reflection

As I have said throughout this chapter, it is essential to keep the preceding verses in view as we read this passage. The Numbers narrative holds the key to understanding the rhetoric that follows. In that light, we understand *κρίσις* to be the

---

[107] cf 1 John 4:18, where "Fear has to do with *discipline*". The NIV translates the word *κόλασις* here as *punishment*, despite the contemporary use of it referring to discipline for the sake of the recipient. (Ramelli and Konstan, *Eternity*, 67.)

[108] In John 7 and 11 we see the Sanhedrin plotting because they see the signs and wonders and, rather than seek to protect the people from a false prophet, the primary fear is that Jesus really *is* the messiah and their political power and authority could be taken from them.

[109] Morris, *John*, 208. See also Carson, *John*, 209; and Harris, *John*, 80.

[110] Tertullian, *ACC*, 129: *"On The Dress of Women" 2.13.*

snake venom that was killing the people in the camp and Jesus as the serpent on the pole being raised up to bring healing. In that light *κρίσις* is something that has happened already and is the inevitable result of sin.

As Paul tells us in Romans 6:23, "For sin's wages are death (*θάνατος*); but God's bestowal of grace is the life (*ζωή*) of the Age (*αἰώνιος*) in the Anointed, Jesus our Lord."[111] Sin kills us. That is what it does. Paul's statement mirrors the story in Numbers 21 and this passage in John. The sin of the people had resulted in the plague of snakes which were killing them, but God's gift offers them healing, salvation and life.

What is notable is that verses 16-18 are about *believing* in Jesus, or not, and the consequences of that choice. Verses 19-21, however, are specifically about the *deeds* of a person. Nothing in this text would suggest that this is in some way *code* for belief or unbelief. As Brian Zahnd notes, "we need to recognise that Jesus uses the word *wicked* in the conventional sense: the wicked are those who live wicked lives, inflicting evil upon others. Jesus does not use the word as a technical term for all of humanity except those who have 'accepted Jesus into their hearts.'"[112]

In addressing the religious rulers, Jesus accuses them of evil deeds, and asserts that it is that very evil that stops them coming to him and being healed. They could see the light. They even recognised it for what it was and chose to stay away from it. This is not a parallel to someone who has seen a distorted version of Jesus through the church and rejected what they saw. Indeed, it is someone who, when faced with the pure reality of Jesus, knowing who he is, chooses to ignore him.

Clearly, there is an eschatological element. Jesus *will* return, the Age to come *will* come and there must be justice for those who have been persecuted, oppressed

---

[111] Hart, *Testament*, 300.
[112] Zahnd, *Sinners*, 126.

Κρίσις in John 3:17-21

and who have suffered. However, as I noted earlier, Salmond asserts that, while John "does not preclude the future judgment which is ascribed to [Jesus] in the Synoptical records", this Gospel speaks of judgment as a "present process."[113]

My findings lead me to doubt any reading of this particular passage (John 3:17-21) as a warning about future condemnation. Taken in its correct context, this passage seems to describe the nature of *κρίσις* as the *consequence* of sin, and not the punishment for it, and as something that has already happened. Jesus did not come to bring *κρίσις* but to free us from it. This passage is not a threat to believe "or else," but an invitation to be freed from death.

---

[113] Salmond, *Immortality,* 260.

CHAPTER FIVE
ΚΡΙΣΙΣ IN JOHN 5:21-30

"Just as the father raises the dead and make them live, so the Son makes alive those whom he wishes; For the Father does not judge anyone but has given the judgment of all to the Son. That all may honour the Son as they honour the Father who sent him. Amen, amen, I tell you that whoever hears my word and has faith in the one who has sent me has the life in the Age, and does not come to judgment, but rather has crossed out of death into life. Amen, amen, I tell you that an hour is coming – and now is – when the dead will hear the voice of the Son of God, and those who hear will live. For as the Father has life in himself, he also granted it to the Son to have life in himself. And he gave power to pass judgment, because he is the Son of Man. Do not be amazed at this, for an hour is coming in which all those in the tombs will hear his voice, And those who have done good things will come forth into a resurrection of life, and those who have done evil things, into a resurrection of judgment. Of myself I can do nothing: I judge as I hear, and my judgment is just, because I see not my will, by rather the will of the one who sent me."

Chapter 5 begins with Jesus healing a man who had been crippled for thirty-eight years and sending him on his way, carrying the mat that he had been living on for years (5-9). This took place on the Sabbath and thus attracted an outcry from the religious leaders (10-13)[114] who demanded to know by what authority Jesus was doing these things (16). What follows is Jesus response, in which he makes several incendiary claims concerning his relationship to the Father and the authority this brings. It is within this context, where "the whole stress is… on the

---

[114] It was the fact that he was carrying his mat that upset them. These are clearly people who need to get out more!

unity of the Father and Son,"[115] that the judgment rhetoric takes place and so we should read and interpret this passage, not as one *about* judgment, but about the divinity and authority of Jesus, in which the issue of judgment is addressed as part of his authentication.

John 5:21-23

"Just as the father raises the dead and make them live, so the Son makes alive those whom he wishes; For the Father does not judge anyone but has given the judgment of all to the Son. That all may honour the Son as they honour the Father who sent him."

Jesus makes two shocking claims about himself in the opening verses of this passage that outraged the religious leaders. First, as Morris notes, "The Father (he and no other) raises people from the dead and gives them life. This is the teaching of the Old Testament (Deut. 32:39; 1 Sam. 2:6; 2 Kings 5:7). It would have been accepted without question by Jesus' hearers,"[116] and so for Jesus to make the claim that *he* will resurrect people would have been appalling to his hearers. While the Jewish leaders were clearly familiar with Elisha raising the boy from death (2 Kings 4), there would be no doubt that the boy eventually died, whether from old age or other causes, but the idea of resurrection to the Age to come was permanent and would never end in death. Jesus was not claiming to raise people in the power of God's Spirit, but in his own power and authority. Cyril of Alexandria lays out clearly the implications of this; "See again in these words clear proof of His Equality. For He That worketh equally in respect of the reviving of the dead, how can He have inferiority in ought?"[117]

---

[115] Morris, *John*, 279.
[116] Morris, *John*, 278-279. See footnote 67 on the same page, where he notes the Rabbinic saying that "three keys are given to the hand of God, and they are not given into the hand of any other agent, namely that of the rain (Deut 28:12), that of the womb (Gen 30:22) and that of the raising of the dead." See also Carson, *John*, 253.
[117] Cyril, *John 2*, 6.

Jesus' opponents understood (correctly) that Jesus was claiming equality with God. And then Jesus continues to goad them by saying that he has authority to judge. Once again, he is taking upon himself the "divine prerogative,"[118] a claim which Keener (in a rather understated manner) notes, "would have unnerved his opponents."[119] They knew without question that *only* YHWH judges and would have "expected to stand before him on the last day."[120] The idea that the very one who stood before them, who was performing miracles—the one whom they were persecuting—was making the clear claim that it would be he, not the Father, who would judge them, must have left them terrified or infuriated. The dilemma they now faced was outlined in Jesus challenge to honour the Father by honouring the Son. They were happy to honour YHWH in a somewhat abstract manner, especially as it gave them power and influence, but it was a whole different prospect when he stood before them, alive, very real and destroying their assumptions and categories.

John 5:24

"Amen, amen, I tell you that whoever hears my word and has faith in the one who has sent me has the life in the Age, and does not come to judgment, but rather has crossed out of death into life."

Hear (ἀκούω) is far more than just having heard something, but, as Harris notes, "ἀκούω means, 'hear and pay heed to/be obedient to'… [and] shows that the 'hearer' and the 'believer' are one and the same person,"[121] and they have crossed into the *life of the Age* discussed in chapter 2 (3:16). Keener asserts that, "one already abides in death until believing in the one who sent Jesus,"[122] suggesting that the move from death to life is *now*, and Harris presents a similar view, arguing

---

[118] Harris, *John*, 113.
[119] Keener, *John 1*, 651.
[120] Morris, *John*, 279.
[121] Harris, *John*, 113.
[122] Keener, *John 1*, 652.

that idea of *crossing over* indicates "'change' one's state or condition."[123] Both of which strongly point to 5:24 being a reprise of 3:16 and the overall idea of being rescued from a current state of sickness or lostness (*spiritual death*) to life of the Age to come.

Morris notes that it is unusual in John's Gospel for Jesus to call hearers to "believe the one who sent me", as opposed to "believe *in* me," which is the norm in the Fourth gospel, with *Jesus* the "object of faith… [rather] than the Father." As the whole discourse is about establishing the oneness of the Father and the Son, it would seem sensible to conclude that this change of emphasis reinforces this point.[124]

John 5:25-27

"Amen, amen, I tell you that an hour is coming – and now is – when the dead will hear the voice of the Son of God, and those who hear will live. For as the Father has life in himself, he also granted it to the Son to have life in himself. And he gave power to pass judgment, because he is the Son of Man."

Several scholars argue for v.25 as a reiteration of v.24, among them C. J. Wright, who argues that "it should be manifest to every reader, not wholly devoid of historical imagination, that by 'dead' the Evangelist neither means those who are physically dead nor the completely annihilated…[but] those who are in need of spiritual quickening."[125] This is a view shared by Chrysostom[126] and Harris, who holds that the dead "refers primarily to those who by nature are unresponsive to

---

[123] Harris, *John,* 114.
[124] Morris, *John*, 280. Although, as we see in 12:44, the two are one and the same.
[125] C. J. Wright, *Jesus the Revelation of God* (London: Hodder & Stoughton, 1950).
[126] John Chrysostom, "Homilies of the Gospel of John," *Documenta Catholica Omnia*, 31 May 2006, <http://www.documentacatholicaomnia.eu/03d/0345-0407,_Iohannes_Chrysostomus,_Homilies_on_The_Gospel_Of_John,_EN.pdf> (6 Feb 2018), 39:2.

God because of their sins."[127] Similarly, Tertullian held the view, reminiscent of Ezekiel 37, that the *dead* in v.25 refers to *the flesh*, asking; "What is the dead thing, if not the flesh?"[128]

Morris disputes this view, arguing that "the language of 28-29 seems too strong for [a view of *the dead* being 'spiritually dead']" and states that "the plain meaning of these words is that he will be our judge on the great Day of Judgement."[129] He does, however (somewhat paradoxically) claim that the phrase "has now come" should make us see that "what is primarily in mind is the present giving of life that characterizes the ministry of the Son,"[130] Carson seems to see "has now come" as a foreshadowing, but with the *emphasis* on the final day, stating that, "the resurrection life for the physically dead in the end time is already being manifest as life for the spiritually dead."[131]

The general (if not unanimous) consensus leans toward the idea that Jesus is referring to the "spiritually dead" in this verse and that the emphasis is on calling them to life, but with the backdrop of the final resurrection. As we will see, this rhetoric builds toward the bigger picture but, at this stage, Jesus is apparently accusing the religious leaders of being "dead." Keener notes "that God's voice brings life would not surprise Jesus' hearers, though such a claim for a human voice would sound jarring,"[132] particularly when Jesus later accuses them of never having heard God's voice (5:37). Again, this language emphasises the main point of the passage – the unity of Father and Son – and it is no coincidence that in this

---

[127] Harris, *John,* 114.
[128] Tertullian, "On the Resurrection of the Flesh," *Tertullian.org,* 19 Feb 2003, <http://www.tertullian.org/articles/evans_res/evans_res_04english.htm> (6 Feb 2018), 37:8.
[129] Morris, *John,* 281.
[130] Morris, *John,* 282.
[131] Carson, *John,* 256.
[132] Keener, *John 1,* 653.

section Jesus refers to himself as "the Son of God"[133] and not his usual *Son of Man*.

The "Son of God" designations helps us stay focused on the purpose of this passage, which, again, is the authority and divinity of Jesus. In the following verses, he goes on to state that the life of the Father is granted to him (26), which Harris interprets as "neither Father or Son is dependent on anything outside himself."[134] And then Christ reasserts his authority to judge on behalf of the Father (27). The claim that "the final verdict on the entire human race is in the hands of one judge alone,"[135] and that judge is Jesus, further shocks Jesus' hearers, which is when Jesus offends them even further with the following verses.

John 5:28-30

"Do not be amazed at this, for an hour is coming in which all those in the tombs will hear his voice, And those who have done good things will come forth into a resurrection of life, and those who have done evil things, into a resurrection of judgment. Of myself I can do nothing: I judge as I hear, and my judgment is just, because I see not my will, but rather the will of the one who sent me."

No longer does the phrase "has now come" feature, which points towards the Day of Judgment, the day that separates this present age from the age to come. As Keener notes, "The future form of 5:28 ('an hour is coming') without the present (cf. 5:25) shows that John's eschatology is not fully realised."[136] This is what Jesus has been building up to all along; the retelling of the religious leaders' own expectations but with *them* as the ones facing judgment, and this judgment by the very one whom they themselves are attempting to judge.

---

[133] This is one of only three times in John when he calls himself this (cf 10:36 and 11:4).
[134] Harris, *John,* 114.
[135] Morris, *John,* 283.
[136] Keener, *John 1,* 654-5.

Κρίσις in John 5:21-30

Once again, despite his repeated claim that those who believe will have the life of the Age (3:16, 5:24,25), Jesus returns to *who have done good and who have done evil* (cf.3:20). This is the first time that this concept is linked with the final judgment in John, but it fits closely to Matthew 25:34,41, and seems to cause some consternation with scholars. Morris states that "this does not mean that salvation is on the basis of good works,"[137] and Carson states, "John is not juxtaposing salvation by works with salvation by faith."[138] Both of these statements are in danger of a theological need to claim that the text does not say what it says. According to Michaels, "a final judgement on the basis of works...was an integral part of Jewish expectation of the end,"[139] so what Jesus was telling the religious leaders was very familiar to them, except that "it is the voice of the Son that will call the dead from their graves."[140] Likewise, Keener states that "Jewish texts were explicit that the wicked would have no part in the 'resurrection to life'" and "that [YHWH] would judge each person according to that person's deeds was a commonplace of both early Jewish and Christian teaching…"[141]

That can seem to confuse things and several questions need asking in response. If salvation is not by works but by *trusting* in Jesus, then does this contradict Jesus' clear assertion or are we missing something about the judgment described? Perhaps Jesus is using their own frame of reference on the Day of Judgment to confront them, challenging their assumption that they are the "ones who have done good." They had used, and continued to use, this assumption to control and oppress the people of Israel, but Jesus confronts them with the reality that they are the ones "who have done evil" and will face *κρίσις*. I will examine this in more depth in the following chapter.

---

[137] Morris, *John*, 285.
[138] Carson, *John*, 259.
[139] Michaels, *John*, 93.
[140] Morris, *John*, 284.
[141] Keener, *John 1*, 655.

Reflection

Keener claims that, distinct from the Synoptic Gospels, whose focus was on "what Jesus did and said," John's main emphasis was "to tell us who Jesus was and what he meant."[142] He proclaims that Christ is one with the Father and has all his authority to act both now and in the end, as the main issue, and it would be a mistake to dissect this section, focussing on each verse out of this context, form a theology from each, and miss the metanarrative of the passage.

Before them stands *YHWH himself*, whom they proport to serve, and yet (as we saw in 3:20) they knowingly oppose and persecute him for fear of losing their own powerbase. In confronting them as he does, Jesus exposes them as deliberately hiding from the light in order to maintain their deception, and thus their own wickedness.

His point in talking about *κρίσις* is to challenge them to see that *he* has unity and life with the Father and it is *his voice* that will call them from their graves and it is *he* who will sit as judge. Once again (as in 3:17-21) Jesus essentially accuses the Jewish rulers of wickedness and warns them of the consequences. On this occasion, he uses their own template of eschatology to do so.

As we have previously noted, *κρίσις* in John is mostly focused on the "present aspect of judgment,"[143] and that the "eschatology of the Synoptic Gospels... occupy a smaller space in John's writings."[144] However, the idea of the Last Day is still there, yet the definition of eschatological *κρίσις* is not given to us in John's gospel, only that the one *who will judge no one* (8:15), will be the evaluator on that day.[145] This may all be less clear cut than we would like, but it is what John gives

---

[142] Keener, *John 1*, 79.
[143] Morris, *John*, 284.
[144] Salmond, *Immortality*, 395.
[145] To find any kind of definition one must look to Matthew 25:46 where it is stated that the wicked will go to αἰώνιον κόλασιν, normally translated as "eternal punishment." However, as we have established in previous chapters, αἰώνιον can better be rendered as "of the Age,"

us. Perhaps as we explore the next section on *κρίσις* in John, we can begin to form a clearer picture.

---

referring to the Age to come (Ramelli & Konstan, *Eternity*, 237). According to the Philosopher Aristotle (*Rhetoric* 1369b13), *Κόλασιν*, which appears only twice in the New Testament "is inflicted in the interest of the sufferer," and not, "in the interest of him who inflicts it, that he may obtain satisfaction." (Ramelli & Konstan, *Eternity*, 67. See also, Hart, *Testament*, 54, footnote). The nature of the Last Day *κρίσις*, according to Matthew can be translated that the wicked will be sent to "discipline of the Age," a phrase implying a redemptive outcome. This is a view held by contemporary theologians such as Robin Parry, (Robin A. Parry, *A Universalist View*, John G. Stackhouse Jr, Robin A. Parry, Jerry L. Walls Denny Burk, *Four Views on Hell* (ed. Preston Sprinkle; : Zondervan, 2016), 116, 117), Thomas Talbott (Thomas Talbott, *The Inescapable Love of God* (Eugene: Cascade Books, 2014), see chapter *Eschatological Punishment*, 75-101), and Brad Jersak (Bradley Jersak, *Her Gates Will Never Be Shut* (Wipf & Stock, 2009)). This was a widely held view among the Early Church Fathers, known as *apocatastasis*. "Origen was a convinced and explicit defender of the idea of apocatastasis, that is, the belief that, after the resurrection and, judgment, and due purification, all human beings would be saved, and evil would be wholly abolished." (Ramelli & Konstan, *Eternity*, 116.) Gregory of Nyssa, likewise, was a proponent of this view, stating that "the punishment by fire is not, therefore, an end in itself, but… the very reason of its infliction is to separate the good from evil in the soul. "(Kevin Knight, "Apocatastisis ," *New Advent*, 2017, <http://newadvent.org/cathen/01599a.htm> (8 Feb 2018)). Clement of Alexandria, also, was convinced of this theology, stating, "God's punishments are saving and disciplinary, leading to conversion, and choosing rather the repentance than the death of a sinner" (Str VI, Clement of Alexandria, "Mercy Upon All," *Mercy Upon All*, 2016, <http://www.mercyuponall.org/tag/clement-of-alexandria/> (16 November 2017)).

CHAPTER SIX

ΚΡΙΣΙΣ IN JOHN 12:44-50

"Jesus spoke aloud and said, 'Whoever has faith in me has faith not in me but in him who has sent me. And whoever sees me sees him who has sent me. I have come as a light into the cosmos, so that everyone who has faith in me might not remain in darkness. And if anyone hears my words and does not keep them I do not judge him; for I came not that I might judge the cosmos, but that I might save the cosmos. Whoever rejects me and does not accept my words has one who judges him: the word that I uttered – that will judge him on the last day. For I did not speak from myself, but rather from the Father who has sent me, he has commanded what I should say and what I should speak. And I know that his command is life in the Age. Thus, whatever things I speak, just as the Father has told me, so I speak." - John 12:44-50

John 12:42,43

In chapter 12, Jesus has arrived in Jerusalem on a borrowed donkey (12:14) for his "triumphal entry", a voice from the heavens has endorsed him (12:28-29) (dismissed by many as "thunder") and then Jesus has performed many miracles. But despite this, most people did not or *would* not believe in him (12:37). What follows in vv.44-50 is Jesus' final public speech in the Fourth Gospel. In the verses preceding John gives us an important insight:

"Many even among the leaders believed in him. But because of the Pharisees they would not openly acknowledge their faith for fear they would be put out of the synagogue; for they loved human praise more than praise from God." (NIV)

Κρίσις in John 12:44-50

It is crucial for us to spend some time on these two verses before examining the discourse itself, because it is not a coincidence that John has made a point of mentioning them, indeed, "the sombre reference to these secret (and therefore false) believers in such a strategic place, right at the end of his summary of Jesus' public ministry, suggests the narrator assigns to them special importance."[146] Morris has a more generous opinion of them, suggesting that their faith was genuine,[147] and Harris describes their faith as "immature or tentative" but notes that their love of the glory of men, should be literally rendered, "'they valued…more than' = 'they much preferred…over',"[148] which calls Morris's view into question. Both Keener[149] and Harris[150] note that John likely has Nicodemus in mind as the example when he makes this statement.

On the balance, I am inclined to see these believers as *false* believers, "whose failure to confess Jesus openly… contrasts starkly with the boldness of the witness, John the Baptist, in 1:20. Loving one's own honour, like loving the world (1 John 2:15) or one's life (John 12:25) demonstrated inadequate love for God and his agent,"[151] and who "still knew nothing of the powerful new birth that could make them children of God."[152] Much of what is said is a repeat of John 3, when Jesus was alone with Nicodemus and John 5, when Jesus responds to the Jewish Leaders about his authority, and I want to argue that their prominence in the narrative, just before this final discourse, is because the words are aimed primarily at them. As such, I think we need to keep this clearly in mind while examining the text.

---

[146] Michaels, *John*, 233. He describes them as having "pseudo faith" and compares them with those mentioned in 2:23 and 8:30,31.

[147] Morris, *John*, 538

[148] Harris, *John*, 238.

[149] Craig S. Keener, *The Gospel of John - A Commentary Volume 2* (Baker Academic, 2012), 884.

[150] Harris, *John*, 238. He also includes Joseph of Arimathea in this.

[151] Keener, *John 2*, 885.

[152] Carson, *John*, 451.

Michaels suggests that this passage (44-50) is a collection of "'leftover' sayings"[153] from John, but Keener insists that the repetition of Jesus' previous teaching is "extremely significant" because it is "summarising and epitomising the message of Jesus in the Gospel to that point."[154] Carson similarly sees this section as a "summarising paragraph powerfully drawing Jesus' public ministry to a close."[155] And as Morris notes, they were spoken *loudly* which he suggests "is probably a way of indicating their importance."[156]

John 12:44-46

"Jesus spoke aloud and said, 'Whoever has faith in me has faith not in me but in him who has sent me. And whoever sees me sees him who has sent me. I have come as a light into the cosmos, so that everyone who has faith in me might not remain in darkness."

Here we see many of the themes repeated from John 5:24, as John uses a "well-known Jewish maxim that 'The person sent is as the one who sent him'"[157] to reinforce the God-given authority of the Son. In the light of this, Keener suggests that "Jesus is God's agent… believing in him is believing in the father and is essential to genuine faith in the Father… [and this] functions as a summons to secret 'believers' in the synagogue."[158] This is the challenge: they claim to worship YHWH; they *know* who Jesus really is, but they will not acknowledge that or fully trust in him and therefore they do not *really* worship YHWH at all. Just as "one dare not be ashamed to confess God in the Shema, one dare not be ashamed to confess Jesus,"[159] and here lies the crux of the speech. He is not challenging those who do

---

[153] Michaels, *John,* 235.
[154] Keener, *John 2,* 886.
[155] Carson, *John,* 451.
[156] Morris, *John,* 539.
[157] Harris, *John,* 239. Cf 13:20.
[158] Keener, *John 2,* 887.
[159] Keener, *John 2,* 887.

not know who he is, but those who *do* know who he is but will not act on it out of pride or selfish reasons.

Jesus (and John to his readers) makes it clear that worshiping YHWH in the synagogue while refusing to acknowledge that he is there before them is not an option. It must be one or the other because "the person who looks on me is at the same time and in reality actually looking on the One who sent me."[160] Thus, to reject Jesus *is* to reject YHWH. As Morris notes, the "'I' is emphatic (repeated in vv. 47,49, 50),"[161] further driving home the point that to follow YHWH you *must* trust Christ. The issue is that these Jewish leaders, characterised by Nicodemus, *knew* who he was and yet were trying to play both sides, clinging to their privileges as the ruling power. Jesus reiterates the statement from 3:19, that he is *the light* and that to *choose* to stay in the darkness is κρίσις itself—exactly as these Pharisees were doing.

John 12:47-48

"And if anyone hears my words and does not keep them I do not judge him; for I came not that I might judge the cosmos, but that I might save the cosmos. Whoever rejects me and does not accept my words has one who judges him: the word that I uttered – that will judge him on the last day."

Again, Jesus makes it clear that he has not come to judge but that his purpose is to save, as we saw in John 3:17. But as Keener notes, "his coming marks a dividing line of judgement."[162] To believe and yet ignore his words (which "were epitomized in his overall message"[163]) was to choose to stay in the darkness and that itself was κρίσις. Not only that, but to reject Jesus while hiding behind the illusion of following "the Father's previous word in the Torah... which testified to Jesus... [when] Jesus'

---

[160] Harris, *John*, 239.
[161] Morris, *John*, 540.
[162] Keener, *John 2*, 888.
[163] Harris, *John*, 239.

word is in fact the same as the Father's word,"[164] was to reject the God whom they profess to serve.

To *knowingly* refuse to act on what they knew to be true would bring *κρίσις* and the measure would be their own hypocrisy. The fact that they *hear* his word means more than just hearing the words but means *understanding* them and recognising what they mean.[165] As a result, their lives would be evaluated against what they knew – Jesus' word – and their duplicity means they have chosen to place themselves among those who act wickedly (5:29) and face *κρίσις*.

John 12:49,50

"For I did not speak from myself, but rather from the Father who has sent me, he has commanded what I should say and what I should speak. And I know that his command is life in the Age. Thus, whatever things I speak, just as the Father has told me, so I speak."

> "The final words of Jesus' public ministry contain a renewed note of certainty. The Father's commandment is no harsh restriction; on the contrary, it is 'eternal life'. It does not simply speak of eternal life nor is it the case that it leads to eternal life ... The commandment *is* eternal life."[166]

Keener asserts that within Johannine texts, "'command' should not be incompatible with believing in Jesus, which is the basis for eternal life."[167] As John concludes Jesus' public ministry he finishes with the words, *"so I speak,"* which Michaels asserts points to the future.[168] Morris claims that the phrase, *"has told me,"* is in the perfect tense and "stresses the permanence of the message, while the

---

[164] Keener, *John 2*, 888.
[165] See notes on 5:24 in previous chapter.
[166] Morris, *John*, 541.
[167] Keener, *John 2*, 889.
[168] Michaels, *John*, 235.

present, 'I say' indicates that Jesus continues right to this moment to speak in this way."[169]

Reflection

John has emphasised the presence of Jewish leaders who believe (in the Western understanding of the word) what Jesus says, but who refuse to believe (πιστευο) in him because of the cost. These are the religious leaders of the Jewish people. These are the men who are the most well versed in the scriptures and have the most influence and power. Tellingly, these are the men who, even under the current Roman occupation, are comfortable, relatively wealthy and somewhat corrupt.

Once again, Jesus warns them of the danger of their hypocrisy. They seem to believe they can continue in the life that they have, superficially worshipping YHWH, and that this will be sufficient for them to be among those who have done good at the final *κρίσις*. Jesus, throughout this passage, uses language that cuts to the heart of their error: To have faith in him is *how* you have faith in the Father; to hear his word *is* to hear the Father's word; his words *are* the Father's words; the fact that you k*now* this and will not act on it is the very thing that brings *κρίσις* upon you.

Again, one cannot form a theological view of *κρίσις* with integrity, or do justice to this passage, by pulling out individual verses out of context. Again, John does not give us any information about the consequences of *κρίσις* on the Last Day, but we cannot ignore the fact that this teaching is aimed at a specific group among the Jewish leaders and clearly seems to challenge them in their falsity.

---

[169] Morris, *John,* 541.

CHAPTER SEVEN

SUMMARY OF FINDINGS AND APPLICATION

When I set out to write this thesis, the question I wanted to answer came from the final chapter of Brad Jersak's book, *Her Gates Will Never Be Shut*, in which he laments, "Most grievously, I am troubled by those evangelicals who ask, 'If hell doesn't exist... why bother being a Christian?' The envy of hedonism and need for fear is all too apparent in such remarks."[170] I personally heard that very question from a minister as I wrote this chapter!

I remember being a teenager who had just become a Christian and my friend telling me that the ideal time to become a Christian was just before you die, but that you just don't know when that will be. I was nineteen and choosing to embrace Christianity had taken two years because, to me, it entailed a long list of things I was going to have to give up. Without a doubt, I *absolutely* envied hedonism and, frankly, fear of hell was the only reason I became a Christian. But "fear is no good reason to believe in anything."[171]

As was noted in the introduction, this motivation undergirds much of the evangelism in the church today.[172] As we said before, this may not be a bad motivation, but is it a *biblical* motivation? Is *the gospel* "get this ticket to heaven"? In looking at John's Gospel I sought to reflect on this question by studying John 3:16 as a summary of the gospel message, and by investigating three

---

[170] Jersak, *Gates,* 186. It should be noted that Jersak is *not* saying that hell does not exist.
[171] Crowder, *Praise the Lord* (2016).
[172] In 2016, within the UK, a movement known as *The Turning* was being heralded as revival. It revolved around the use of a "script" which was read to people on the streets. One of the opening sentences of the script was "if you die today, do you know for sure that you will go to heaven?" (Revival Ministries International, *The Gospel Soul-Winning Script* (n.d.)) This script, we were told *is the gospel.*

discourses on judgment within the book. I examined the Greek terms, the contexts and the content of each of these sections to see what place judgment, and thus fear, plays in the gospel presentation. I have focused on the meaning of *αἰώνιος ζωή* as the invitation, and in more depth, on *κρίσις* as the consequence of refusing the invitation.

John 3:16 and *Αἰώνιος ζωή*

The research into John 3:16 has shown that extracting it from the context of the preceding verses leads us to miss something significant from the Numbers 21 story. Namely, that the invitation is to *αἰώνιος ζωή,* an offer of rescue from a *present* condition of *lostness* or state of perishing. Conversely, it is not an ultimatum between "salvation or judgment,"[173] or a threat of future punishment.

I have shown that the very concept of *αἰώνιος ζωή* is of *life of the future age now,* and not code for *life after death,* or *heaven*. The invitation is to partake in something beautiful right now—to enter into life as it was always meant to be. The life that we were always created to live. This being the case, the idea of being jealous of hedonism becomes almost absurd, as such a lifestyle can only be a futile attempt to capture the fullness of life that is *αἰώνιος ζωή,* which we were created for in the first place.

For us, therefore, to reduce the gospel to a way of avoiding hell, the benefits of which will not be seen before death, is problematic. To be blunt, if the gospel *is* just about going to heaven then the most loving thing that one could do after leading someone to Christ would be to dispatch them to meet their Maker and let them begin reaping the benefits of their conversion. But that is not *αἰώνιος ζωή* and it is not the invitation of John 3:16.

---

[173] Alan Charles Blackwood, "The Theology of Judgement in the Fourth Gospel - Christology and Eschatology in John 5," *University of Glasgow*, July 2005, <http://theses.gla.ac.uk/983/1/2005blackwoodphd.pdf> (16 November 2017), 58.

Summary of Findings and Application

If we can summarise the Gospel invitation from what we read in John 3:16, then it would be "God showed us how much he loved the cosmos by sending his only Son. All you need do is trust him and you will be rescued from spiritual death and begin the new life of the Age to come."[174]

Κρίσις in the Gospel of John

In researching into the use of *κρίσις*, it became apparent that the meaning of this word is not as clear-cut as the modern church would assert, namely, *condemnation*. I have shown that in its use within the Septuagint, and especially the Torah, it is almost never used to mean that. It was almost exclusively used to mean *decide* or *evaluate* (in the context of a judge hearing a person's case). With that being the case, if we read the familiar passages that talk of judgment, we should remove the filter of *κρίσις* always meaning *condemnation* and try to read *κρίσις* as *evaluating*. It is notable that some scholars appear to translate *κρίσις* as either *judgment* or *condemnation*, often within the same sentence or passage, to fit into a pre-existing theological framework.[175]

In studying the three passages about *κρίσις* in the Fourth Gospel – John 3:17-19; 5:24-29 and 12:44-50 – two things have become clear. First, most theologians agree that John differs from the Synoptics in his focus on judgment *in this age*. And while scholars note the predominant *present* nature of the judgment there is consensus that it is not *exclusively* present, containing some eschatological elements, and does not in any way contradict the Synoptic view. Second, that all these discourses are addressed to members of the Jewish ruling council and the fact that members of the Sanhedrin were recipients of the judgment warnings from Jesus. This is cause for us to pause and take note.

---

[174] Harris argues that the invitation to believe/trust "could be rendered, 'everyone who at any time believes,'" and that "the promise remains valid for all time." Harris, *John,* 78.
[175] Morris, *John,* 280, cf 284.

Summary of Findings and Application

I have shown that Jesus took the accepted Jewish eschatological framework of the day – that the wicked would have no place in the age to come – and switched the places of the Jewish leaders. To their shock, it was *they* who found themselves "walking in the counsel of the wicked, standing in the place of sinners and sitting in the seat of the scornful" (Ps 1:1). In this context, it becomes more difficult to lift these passages and form a Johannine eschatology and in my view, it would be a mistake to do so.

The Place of *Αἰώνιος ζωή* and *Κρίσις* in the Gospel Invitation

Whatever view one's conviction concerning John's eschatology, we must at least acknowledge that the passages regarding judgment are not in the context of mission but of rebuking, challenging and correcting the corrupt institution of the Judean council. If we look at the proclamation of good news in the thread throughout John, we see invitation, but no mention is made of punishment and no hint of threat is contained. In the public "I am" proclamations,[176] Jesus invites the people into *αἰώνιος ζωή* and never once mentions any form of the final judgment. It is always, as with John 3:16, an invitation to come out of a current state of spiritual hunger (6:35-38), spiritual darkness (8:12), religion (10:1-18), death (11:25) and into *αἰώνιος ζωή*.[177]

---

[176] I have excluded the John 15, "I am the vine" as this was made in private to his disciples.
[177] We may conclude that, within the Fourth Gospel, there is no example of Jesus threatening everlasting punishment to the people if they refuse the invitation. However, it is worth pausing for a moment to briefly mention the Synoptics, because one can rightly make the accusation that just looking at one Gospel in isolation is not enough to form a theology. However, a scan of the Synoptics shows us that, as with John, the threat of eschatological judgment is limited almost exclusively to or about the Jewish leaders. It is never used as a threat to those who would refuse *αἰώνιος ζωή*.
Matt 7:21-23 - for Context, Jesus is comparing the religious way of life offered by the Pharisees (the wide gate) compared with the life he offers (the narrow gate) (Tim Keller, "Gospel in Life Podcast - The Inside Out Kingdom," *Podbean*, 13 Aug 2015, <http://www.podbean.com/media/share/dir-kz8bw-11f0b9a> (7 Feb 2018)) and so by extension his warning is clearly addressed to or about the religious elite. **Matt 12:24-37** has much overlap with John 12:44-50 and, once again, is addressed to the Pharisees. **Matt 25:46** is a private conversation with the disciples and not a public proclamation although it could be

Summary of Findings and Application

It would be foolhardy (and patently wrong) to attempt to assert that *κρίσις* plays no part in the fourth Gospel, but as I have shown, the Evangelist's presentation of Jesus' use of it is limited to his interaction with the Pharisees and is rhetoric to address their own theological prejudices. It is apparent that within the Gospel of John (and arguably the Synoptics too), the invitation to come into *αἰώνιος ζωή* is never countered with the threat of everlasting punishment for those who refuse it, but that the invitation and offer of *αἰώνιος ζωή* stands on its own.

If we, as the followers of Christ, purport to emulate him, we must question why we would feel a need to scare people into conversion when he never did. Whether one agrees with my conclusions on the nature of *κρίσις* it is still clear to see that it did not feature in Jesus' call to the lost. In context, one can assert that the gospel invites all to partake in the *αἰώνιος ζωή* of the Kingdom of God—that message is the same regardless of one's eschatological view. The offer is *αἰώνιος ζωή* right now, right here, and that means a lifetime of discipleship as we await the Age to come.

"This is how God loved the world, he gave the gift of his one and only son, that whoever gives themselves over to him totally, will no longer be lost but will have begun the eternal kind of life from the coming age."

---

argued to refer to the religious leaders in that it has much in common with John 5:24-29 and 12:44-50. **Matt 10:9-15, Luke 10:12ff, Matt 11:20-24.** Wright makes the argument that these passages refer to the choice to take "Jesus' way of peace [and not] the way of violence," which would eventually see them crushed under the Roman Army in AD70 (Tom Wright, *Matthew for Everyone Part 1* (London : SPCK, 2004), 113, 114.) As such, this passage can be seen to not be eschatological at all. In the Synoptics the invitation is to "the kingdom" rather than eternal life but, as mentioned before, is the equivalent. See Michaels, *John*, 59.

BIBLIOGRAPHY

<http://www.tertullian.org/fathers/cyril_on_john_02_book2.htm> (16 November 2017).

—. "The Tertullian Project." *Commentary on John, Book 1* 2005. <http://www.tertullian.org/fathers/cyril_on_john_01_book1.htm> (16 November 2017).

Anglicans Online. "The Nicene Creed." *Anglicansonline.org* May 2017. <http://anglicansonline.org/basics/nicene.html> (28 September 2017).

Athanasius of Alexandria. *On the Incarnation.* Fig books, 2012.Augustine. "Tractate 12." *New Advent* 2017. <http://www.newadvent.org/fathers/1701012.htm> (24 Jan 2018).

Banks, Robert, ed. *Reconciliation and Hope - New Testament Essays on Atonement and Eschatology.* The Paternoster Press Ltd., 1974.

Barth, Karl. "The Extinction of Humanity: Karl Barth's Eschatology." *The PostBarthian* 30 Nov 2016. <https://postbarthian.com/2016/11/30/extinction-humanity-karl-barths-eschatology/> (7 Feb 2018).

Bauer, Walter. *A Greek-English Lexicon of the New Testament and Other Early Christian LIterature.* Edited by William F. Arndt and F. Wilbur Gingrich. Chicago: Univeristy of Chicago Press, 1979.

Beasley-Murray, George. *John (2nd ed.).* Nashville: Thomas Nelson, 1999.

Blackwood, Alan Charles. "The Theology of Judgement in the Fourth Gospel - Christology and Eschatology in John 5." *University of Glasgow* July 2005. <http://theses.gla.ac.uk/983/1/2005blackwoodphd.pdf> (16 November 2017).

Boyd, Greg. "Annihilation." *Dr. Platypus* 21 Aug 2007. <https://pursiful.com/2007/08/21/greg-boyd-annihilation-or-eternal-suffering-1/> (7 Feb 2018).

Caneday, A. B. "The Advent of God's Son as Judgement in John's Gospel: Justification and Condemnation Already." *Credo Magazine* November 2011. <http://www.credomag.com/wp-content/uploads/2011/11/The-Advent-of-God%E2%80%99s-Son-as-Judgment-in-John%E2%80%99s-Gospel-Justification-and-Condemnation-Already.pdf> (16 November 2017).

Carson, D. A. *The Gospel According to John.* Leicester: Apollos, 1991.

Christian Reformed Church. "Nicene Creed." *Christian Reformed Church* n.d.. <https://www.crcna.org/welcome/beliefs/creeds/nicene-creed> (28 September 2017).

Chrysostom, John. "Homilies of the Gospel of John." *Documenta Catholica Omnia* 31 May 2006. <http://www.documentacatholicaomnia.eu/03d/0345-0407,_Iohannes_Chrysostomus,_Homilies_on_The_Gospel_Of_John,_EN.pdf> (6 Feb 2018).

Clement of Alexandria. *Mercy Upon All* 2016. <http://www.mercyuponall.org/tag/clement-of-alexandria/> (16 November 2017).

Crowder. *Praise the Lord.* Comp. David Crowder. 2016.

Cyril of Alexandria. "Commentary on John, Book 2." *The Tertullian Project* 2005.

D.A. Carson, Douglas J. Moo and Leon Morris. *An Introduction to the New Testament.* Apollos, 1992.

Denny Burk, John G. Stackhouse Jr, Robin A. Parry, Jerry L. Walls. *Four Views on Hell.* Edited by Preston Sprinkle. Zondervan, 2016.

Elowsky, Joel C., ed. *Ancient Christian Commentary on Scripture, New Testament IVa, John 1-10.* Illinois: IVP, 2006.

"Eternal Life." *All About Spirituality* n.d.. <https://www.allaboutspirituality.org/eternal-life-faq.htm> (24 Jan 2018).

Evangelical Alliance Commision on Unity and Truth Among Evangelicals. *The Nature of Hell.* London: Paternoster, 2000.

Grudem, Wayne. *Systematic Theology: An Introduction to Biblical Doctrine.* IVP Press & Zondervan Publishing House, 1994.

Harris, Murray J. *John.* Nashville: B&H Academic, 2015.

Hart, David Bentley. *The New Testament: A Translation.* New Haven: Yale University Press, 2017.

Hyam, Matt. *I Still Have More Questions Than Answers.* Vineyard International Publishing, 2004.

Irenaeus. "Irenaeus: Agibst Heresies." *The Gnostic Society Library* n.d.. <http://gnosis.org/library/advh5.htm> (31 January 2018).

Jersak, Bradley. *Her Gates Will Never Be Shut.* Wipf & Stock, 2009.

Keener, Craig S. *The Gospel of John - A commentary Volume 1.* Baker Academic, 2012.

—. *The Gospel of John - A Commentary Volume 2.* Baker Academic, 2012.

Keller, Tim. "Gospel in Life Podcast - The Inside Out Kingdom." *Podbean* 13 Aug 2015. <http://www.podbean.com/media/share/dir-kz8bw-11f0b9a> (7 Feb 2018).

Knight, Kevin. "Apocatastisis ." *New Advent* 2017. <http://newadvent.org/cathen/01599a.htm> (8 Feb 2018).

Konstan, Ilaria L. E. Ramelli & David. *Terms for Eternity: Aionios and Aidios in Classical and Christian Texts.* Piscataway: Gorgias Press LLC, 2013.

Lewis, C. S. *The Last Battle.* Glasgow: Fontana Lions, 1956.

Martin, Ralph P. *New Testament Foundations Vol.1.* Eerdmans, 1975.

Michaels, J. Ramsey. *John.* Massachusetts: Hendrickson, 1989.

Morris, Leon. *The Gospel According to John.* Grand Rapids: Wm. B. Eermanns Publishing C., 1995.

Oxford Dictionaries. "Oxford Living Dictionaries." 2017. <https://en.oxforddictionaries.com> (16 November 2017).

Piper, John. "Are All Sins Equal Before God?" *Desiring God* 2 Nov 2009. <https://www.desiringgod.org/interviews/are-all-sins-equal-before-god> (1 February 2018).

—. "The Destiny: Eternal Life." *Desiring God* 25 Dec 1994. <https://www.desiringgod.org/messages/the-destiny-eternal-life> (24 Jan 2018).

Revival Ministries International. "The Gospel Soul-Winning Script." n.d.

Salmond, Stewart D. F. *The Christian Doctrine of Immortality.* Edinburgh: T. & T. Clark, 1901.

Stott, John. "Judgement and Hell." *Truth According to Scripture* n.d.. <https://www.truthaccordingtoscripture.com/documents/death/judgement-hell.php#.WnsUk6hl_IU> (7 Feb 2018).

Talbott, Thomas. *The Inescapable Love of God.* Eugene: Cascade Books, 2014.

Tertullian. "On the Resurrection of the Flesh." *Tertullian.org* 19 Feb 2003. <http://www.tertullian.org/articles/evans_res/evans_res_04english.htm> (6 Feb 2018).

Thomas, R. L. *New American Standard Hebrew-Aramaic and Greek Dictionaries: updated Edition.* Anaheim: Foundation Publications, inc., 1998.

Westcott, Brooke Foss. *The Epistles of St John.* Cambridge: Macmillan, 1886.

—. *The Gospel According to St John.* John Murray, 1882.

Willard, Dallas. *The Divine Conspiracy.* Harper Collins, 1998.

Wright, C. J. *Jesus the Revelation of God.* London: Hodder & Stoughton, 1950.

Wright, Tom. *Matthew for Everyone Part 1.* London : SPCK, 2004.

—. *Surprised by Hope.* London: SPCK, 2007.

—. *The Day the Revolution Began.* SPCK, 2016.

Zahnd, Brian. *Sinners in the Hands of a Loving God.* Waterbrook Press, 2017.

www.ingramcontent.com/pod-product-compliance
Lightning Source LLC
Chambersburg PA
CBHW052116070526
44584CB00017B/2517